SCIENCE INVESTIGATORS

Investigating WEATHER and CLIMATE Through Modeling

Derek Miller

Cavendish Square
New York

Published in 2020 by Cavendish Square Publishing, LLC
243 5th Avenue, Suite 136, New York, NY 10016

First Edition

Cataloging-in-Publication Data
Names: Miller, Derek.
Title: Investigating weather and climate through modeling / Derek Miller.
Description: New York : Cavendish Square, 2020. | Series: Science investigators | Includes glossary and index.
Identifiers: ISBN 9781502652553 (pbk.) | ISBN 9781502652560 (library bound) | ISBN 9781502652577 (ebook)
Subjects: LCSH: Weather--Juvenile literature. | Climatology--Juvenile literature.
Classification: LCC QC981.3 M55 2020 | DDC 551.5--dc23

Editor: Caitlyn Miller
Copy Editor: Nathan Heidelberger
Associate Art Director: Alan Sliwinski
Designer: Ginny Kemmerer
Production Coordinator: Karol Szymczuk
Photo Research: J8 Media

The photographs in this book are used by permission and through the courtesy of:
Cover, Akimov Igor/Shutterstock.com; p. 4 FotoKina/Shutterstock.com; p. 9 Samuel Lane/Getty Images; p. 10 trekandshoot/Shutterstock.com; p. 12 Fineart1/Shutterstock.com; p. 13 Weather.gov; p. 15 Filip Jedraszak/Shutterstock.com; p. 16 Checubus/Shutterstock.com; p. 17 Cemil Aksoy/Shutterstock.com; p. 20 Ranglen/Shutterstock.com; p. 22 Vitalii Matokha/Shutterstock.com; p. 24 Richard Thorton/Shutterstock.com; p. 25 corbac40/Shutterstock.com; p. 28 9387388673/Shutterstock.com; p. 30 bugdann.t/Shutterstock.com; p. 32 ttsz/iStock/Getty Images; p. 34 robert_s/Shutterstock.com; p. 36 Nickeline/Shutterstock.com; p. 37 BlaineT/Shutterstock.com; p. 39 Evgeny Karandaev/Shutterstock.com.

Printed in the United States of America

Contents

Changes in the weather can have big consequences for people everywhere.

CHAPTER 1

What Are Weather and Climate?

People often confuse weather and climate. The two concepts are related, but there are also key differences between them. Weather is what happens in a short period of time. A place's weather might be rainy or sunny, hot or cold. Climate is the average weather of a place over a much longer time period. A place's climate might cause hot summers and cold winters. Some days might not fit this average. Sometimes, there is a cool day in the summer. The weather on that cool day doesn't change the overall climate, though. Because weather and climate are part of our everyday lives, it's important to learn more about them.

WHAT AFFECTS CLIMATE?

Not everywhere has hot summers and cold winters. Some places have mild temperatures year-round or during a particular season. For example, in Miami, Florida, winters are not very cold at all. Other places are very cold year-round. On the world's tallest mountain, Mount Everest, it can drop below freezing on a summer day. Climates around the world vary a great deal.

Many factors affect the climate of a place. The temperature is mostly the result of warmth from the sun. Different regions receive different amounts of sunlight. The more sunlight a place gets, the hotter it usually is. Still, it is not quite that simple. Currents of air and water circulate, or move, around Earth as well. These currents can carry heat from the sun around the world in strange ways. The huge sheets of ice at the North and South Poles also play a big role in shaping the climate. Sunlight, the oceans, air, and ice all work together to make the different climates around Earth.

The weather on a particular day is mostly the result of air masses. An air mass is a huge body of air. Different air masses have different characteristics. Characteristics of air masses include temperature and humidity. Humidity is how much water vapor is in the air. Air masses also have different pressures. The pressure is the weight of all the air above us pressing down toward Earth. Air pressure, temperature, and humidity cause weather conditions like rain storms, and they affect how hot or cold it feels.

PREDICTING THE WEATHER

Predicting the weather is very difficult. Because so many factors affect the weather, it is impossible to know exactly what will happen next. However, scientists can predict the probability of a weather event. Probability is the chance that something will happen. For example, scientists may predict that there is a 50 percent chance it will rain tomorrow.

The scientists who predict the weather are called meteorologists. Meteorologists use models and data to make predictions. Their predictions are always probabilistic, or based on probability. They don't know for sure that something will happen, but they can determine the chance that it will happen.

PREVENTING DISASTER

Even though weather forecasts are probabilistic, they are very useful. On a typical day, knowing that there is a chance of rain lets people know they should carry an umbrella. In extraordinary circumstances, forecasts can save lives. Predicting the likely path of a hurricane or when a tornado could form lets people get to safety. Scientists design so-called early detection systems to predict tornadoes and tsunamis. Tsunamis are huge waves that can flood entire cities. An early warning gives people time to get to safety.

Engineers also limit the damage that extreme weather causes. Many cities have levees that hold back high water. Levees can be walls or mounds of earth. When storms hit and the water rises, levees stop floods and save lives.

The First Weatherman

In 1859, a terrible storm struck the coast of Great Britain. With no warning to get out of the way of the coming storm, hundreds of sailors lost their lives at sea. Scientist and sailor Robert FitzRoy made up his mind to prevent further disasters at sea. He would try to forecast the weather and warn sailors of storms.

FitzRoy's efforts were made possible by a new invention: the telegraph. Invented in the 1830s, the telegraph sent messages over electrical wires at lightning-fast speeds. This was before telephones and the internet. At the time, most messages were still delivered by horse or carriage.

FitzRoy had coast guard stations around the country send him weather reports by telegraph. Armed with the knowledge of local weather conditions, he tried to predict what would happen next. If a storm was moving up the coast, he could telegraph warnings to ports in its path. The warnings were passed on to local sailors. For the first time, sailors had more information than just looking at the sky to decide if it was safe to go out to sea or not.

Robert FitzRoy's weather reports were published in newspapers around Britain.

These early weather forecasts were quite simple. FitzRoy started by forecasting just two days in the future, and, like today, his forecasts were sometimes wrong. Many people of his time made fun of his efforts. Even other scientists thought he was crazy. Over time, people realized it was possible to make solid weather predictions. Today, FitzRoy is celebrated as the first person to use science to predict the weather.

Las Vegas has a desert climate. People avoid walking around at noon in the summer.

CHAPTER 2

Modeling Climate

A place's climate is very important. It affects many parts of daily life, like the clothes people wear and how they build their houses. The climate also affects what plants and crops will grow somewhere. In the past, people's diets and their work were planned around the climate. Today, the climate of different places affects where people go on vacation and where they choose to live.

CLIMATE DATA

Determining a place's climate is much easier than forecasting the weather. When scientists try to predict the weather, they try to figure out the future. When scientists try to figure out the climate, they look at the past. Looking at past data is much more accurate than predicting how air masses will move in the future.

Modern scientists collect data on the weather minute by minute, as it's happening. This data is recorded at weather stations and used to build a picture of the climate. For example, a weather station in Washington, DC, might track the amount of rain, current temperature, and the number of hours of sunlight each day. Data is collected over many decades. Averaging this

Meteorologists collect data from weather stations.

data gives an accurate picture of what the weather usually looks like in this area in a given month or year.

It is important that scientists gather data over a long time to determine a place's climate. The weather in one year might be extreme. Some years there is much more precipitation than others. Precipitation is rain, snow, hail, or sleet. Other years might be much hotter or colder than usual. By averaging many years together, unusual years don't really skew, or change, the data.

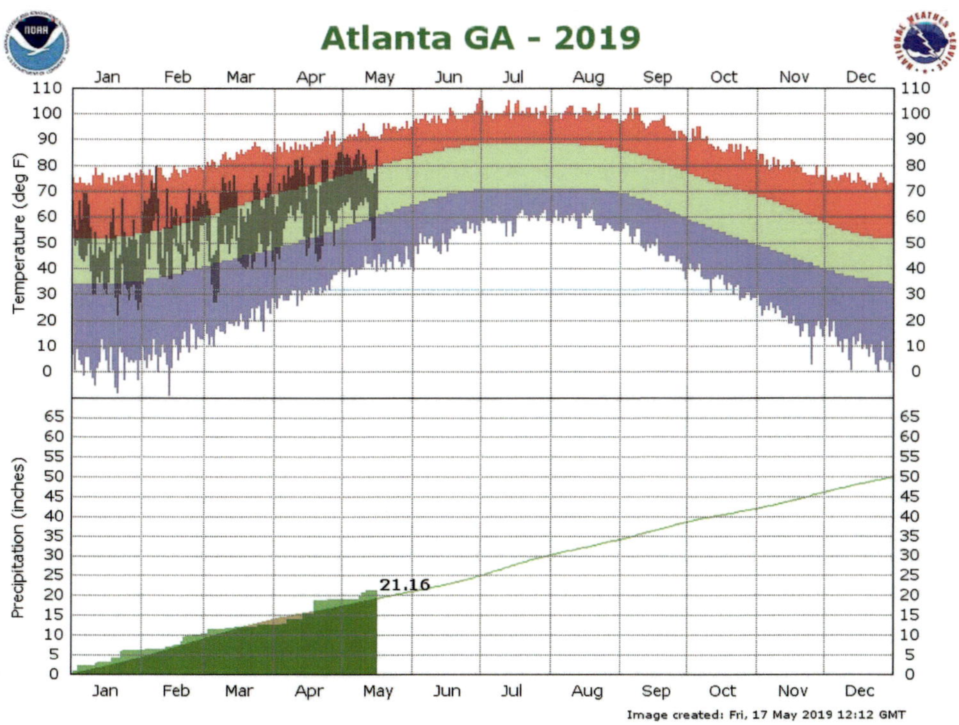

The dark shading shows the actual temperature and precipitation in Atlanta in 2019 through May. The red, green, and blue bands and the line in the lower graph show the past temperatures and precipitation.

MAKE YOUR OWN CLIMATE MODEL

Graphs are a useful model for showing a place's climate. You can use a graph to show average temperatures, precipitation, or hours of sunshine. Climate graphs let someone see at a glance what weather to expect in a given month.

To investigate differences in rainy seasons, we're going to graph the average precipitation of three cities: Los Angeles, New York, and Delhi. Los Angeles and New York are both in the United States, but they have very different patterns of precipitation. Meanwhile, Delhi, India, has an intense rainy season not seen in the United States. This is sometimes called the monsoon season, although "monsoon" is often used to mean wind patterns as well.

Making a Graph

To make this graph, all you need is a sheet of graph paper and four pens, pencils, or markers of different colors. First, pick a color to use to both label your graph and create the graph itself. At the top of the paper, title the graph "average monthly precipitation." A good title lets viewers know what they are looking at. Below your title, pick a line near the left-hand side of your paper and trace a line down forty squares. At the bottom of the last square, trace a line twenty-five squares to the right.

Monsoon season in Delhi can bring flooding due to heavy rainfall.

Label the line going from top to bottom "average inches of precipitation." Write a 0 to the left of the corner of the lines you drew. Going up, count four squares and write the number 1. Keep counting four squares and writing the next number up until you hit 10 at the top.

Label the line running from left to right "month." Under the line, write "January" one line to the right of the line you traced going from top to bottom. Keep going to the right and label every other line the next month of the year. Now, you should have the twelve months labeled on the bottom line and the numbers one through ten labeled on the line running top to bottom.

Plotting the Data

Use the data below to plot points on your graph. This data was gathered by scientists. It is the average precipitation that each city saw over a long period of time. Plot the points for one city and then connect the points using one of your three remaining colors. Use a different color for each city so that you can compare them easily. Be sure to label which color stands for which city.

Los Angeles:

- January: 4 inches
- February: 5 inches
- March: 2.75 inches
- April: 1 inch
- May: 0.25 inch
- June: 0 inches
- July: 0 inches
- August: 0 inches
- September: 0.25 inch
- October: 1 inch
- November: 1.25 inches
- December: 2.75 inches

Los Angeles is known for its sunny climate.

New York City:

- January: 4 inches
- February: 3 inches
- March: 4 inches
- April: 4 inches
- May: 4.5 inches
- June: 3.5 inches
- July: 4.5 inches
- August: 4.25 inches
- September: 4 inches
- October: 3.5 inches
- November: 3.75 inches
- December: 3.5 inches

Snow is common in New York City in the winter.

Delhi:

- January: 0.75 inch
- February: 0.75 inch
- March: 0.5 inch
- April: 0.5 inch
- May: 1 inch
- June: 3 inches
- July: 8.5 inches
- August: 10 inches
- September: 4.75 inches
- October: 0.75 inch
- November: 0.25 inch
- December 0.25 inch

You should have a graph with three different lines of different colors. These lines model the average precipitation each city sees over the course of a year. They may cross and be similar sometimes, but the climate of each city is very different. You can use this climate model to predict what the precipitation will be like in each city in a given month.

Test Yourself

1. Which two months in Los Angeles have the highest precipitation on average?
2. Does New York City have a rainy season?
3. Which of the four seasons is the rainy season in Delhi?
4. Which city has the highest average precipitation in February?
5. Looking at the graph, estimate which city sees the least average precipitation in a year.

Answers:

1. January and February
2. No—precipitation in New York City doesn't change much from month to month.
3. The summer is the rainy season. It rains a lot in July and August.
4. Los Angeles
5. Los Angeles sees less precipitation on average than either New York City or Delhi. No month is very rainy.

Power plants release pollution as they create electricity.

CHAPTER 3

Modeling Climate Change

The climate of a place can change, but this happens very slowly. Average temperatures may rise or fall. Even small changes in the average can have a huge effect. A few degrees might mean the difference between a great deal of snow or very little snow. Differences in weather between one year and the next are not climate change. They are normal variations in weather.

NATURAL CLIMATE CHANGE

Some climate change is natural. Earth's climate goes through cycles. It changes over time. Some periods of Earth's history were colder than average, and some were warmer than average. Colder periods are called glacial periods. Glaciers are huge masses of ice and snow. They exist in places with cold temperatures and can grow or shrink, depending on the amount of snowfall.

Today, glaciers mostly exist near the South Pole and North Pole and very high in the mountains, where it is cold. However, just fourteen thousand years ago, many parts of North America and Europe were covered by glaciers. Almost all of Canada, England, Norway, and Sweden were giant sheets of ice!

Average temperatures at the time were only 10.8 degrees Fahrenheit (6 degrees Celsius) lower than they are today.

Glaciers still cover parts of Iceland.

Still, this small difference had a huge impact on the surface of Earth and its weather. The oceans were much lower at the time because so much of Earth's water was frozen in glaciers.

As Earth began to warm up, woolly mammoths died out. Scientists believe the changing climate affected their food sources. The glaciers retreated, and sea levels rose. Lands that had once been connected became islands. Humans around the world changed how they lived to adapt to the changing climate. Life on Earth changed forever.

HUMANS AND CLIMATE CHANGE

In modern times, humans have contributed to climate change. The average temperature on Earth is rising in a process known as global warming. Natural causes are partly to blame, but humans are also driving global warming. This change in the overall surface and ocean temperatures on Earth is leading to climate change. In fact, global warming can actually cause more extreme winter weather events!

The main way that humans affect the climate is through burning fossil fuels. Natural gas, crude oil, and coal are fossil fuels. Fossil fuels are formed from the remains of plants and animals trapped in Earth's crust. Over millions of years, heat and

Oil wells bring oil from deep underground to Earth's surface.

pressure transform their remains into natural gas, crude oil, and coal.

Fossil fuels are burned to create energy. Much of the world's electricity comes from burning coal, and most vehicles run on fuel made from crude oil—like gasoline. When fossil fuels are burned, they release greenhouse gases, such as carbon dioxide. Carbon dioxide exists naturally in the air we breathe and is usually harmless. However, it also contributes to the greenhouse effect. Carbon dioxide traps heat on Earth just like a greenhouse traps heat inside its glass walls. This means heat from the sun is trapped in Earth's atmosphere by carbon dioxide and other greenhouse gases. The atmosphere is the layer of gas that surrounds Earth and makes life possible.

Since humans began burning fossil fuels, the amount of greenhouse gases has skyrocketed. Average temperatures of Earth have increased as a result. Temperatures will increase more unless humans around the world work together to rely less on fossil fuels.

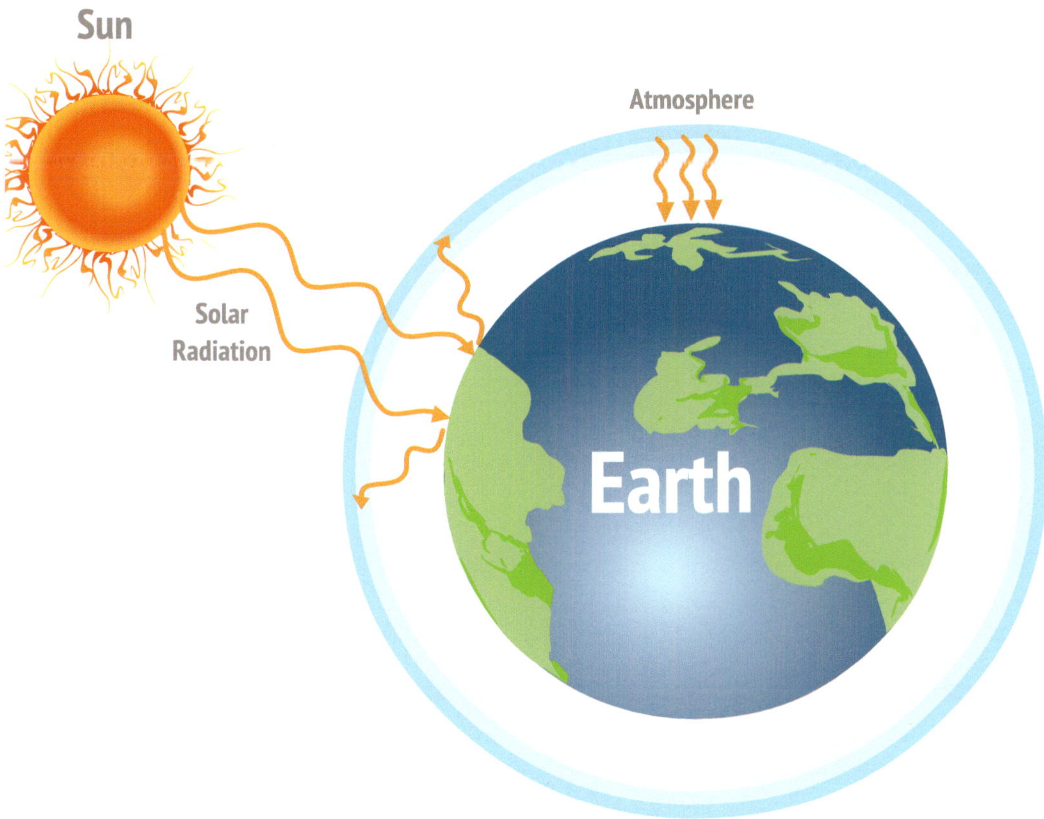

The greenhouse effect is when heat from the sun is trapped by Earth's atmosphere.

MAKING A DIFFERENCE

A carbon footprint is the amount of greenhouse gases that someone is responsible for releasing. Many choices we make every day affect our carbon footprint. For example, turning off the light when we leave a room reduces how much electricity we use. This means a smaller amount of fossil fuels needs to be burned.

Taking a bus or train instead of driving is another way people can reduce their carbon footprint. Public transportation is much better for the planet than driving since many people fit in one bus or train car.

Eating less meat is another choice that reduces a person's carbon footprint. Raising many animals on large farms (called factory farms) releases huge amounts of greenhouse gases. Aside from burning fossil fuels, raising animals is one of the biggest causes of greenhouse gases.

If we don't limit our carbon footprint, climate change will continue. Extreme weather like devastating hurricanes and wildfires will become more common. Droughts, or long dry periods, will cause people to run out of food in parts of the world. Some island nations may even disappear underwater as sea levels rise when glaciers melt.

MAKE YOUR OWN MODEL OF THE GREENHOUSE EFFECT

You can see the effect that greenhouse gases have by building a model. Greenhouse gases got their name because they work much the same way as a greenhouse for growing plants. To build your own greenhouse, all you need is an empty two-liter bottle, something to cut it with, dirt, and a small plant you dug up carefully.

First, peel any labels off the bottle. Then, ask an adult to help you cut it. Stand the bottle up and cut it midway between the top and bottom. Poke a few holes in the bottom so that any extra water can drain out.

Put about 2 inches (5 cm) of dirt into the bottom of the bottle. Hold the plant so that its roots are resting on the dirt, and pour more dirt around it, pressing the dirt down lightly, until the plant stands up on its own. If you don't have a small plant you can dig up, you can get a small potted plant from a store. You can then put the plant and the dirt around its roots into the bottle and just add more dirt around it so that it doesn't fall over.

Water the plant, and then put the top of the bottle over the bottom to cover it. If it doesn't fit well, you can easily tape the

For this model, you can use a small plant you buy from the store or one you've dug up.

two pieces together. Your greenhouse is complete! Make sure the lid of the bottle is on to trap heat and moisture inside, just like Earth's atmosphere traps gas and water. Put the bottle in the sun so that the plant gets plenty of light. If your plant grows big, you can move it out of the bottle to a pot big enough for it.

Test Yourself

1. Is it warmer inside or outside the bottle after it is placed in the sun? If you have a small thermometer, you can place it inside the bottle for a while, record the temperature, and move it outside.
2. In this model, the plastic traps heat in the bottle. On Earth, what traps sunlight close to the planet and is causing climate change?
3. After a few hours in the sun, is there any evidence water is trapped in the bottle?

Answers:

1. It will be warmer inside the bottle than outside of it.
2. greenhouse gases like carbon dioxide in Earth's atmosphere
3. There will likely be drops of water visible on the inside of the plastic bottle. This is the same process that forms clouds and then rain in the sky.

Water from the ocean eventually forms clouds and then rain.

CHAPTER 4

Modeling the Water Cycle

Water plays a huge role in Earth's climate. Precipitation like rain and snow changes the temperature. Oceans change our weather and climate too. Without water, Earth's weather and climate would be very different. Life would not even be possible.

OCEAN CURRENTS

Oceans cover about two-thirds of Earth's surface. It is no surprise that they are very important to weather and climate. Water in the ocean is constantly moving. Ocean currents move water in

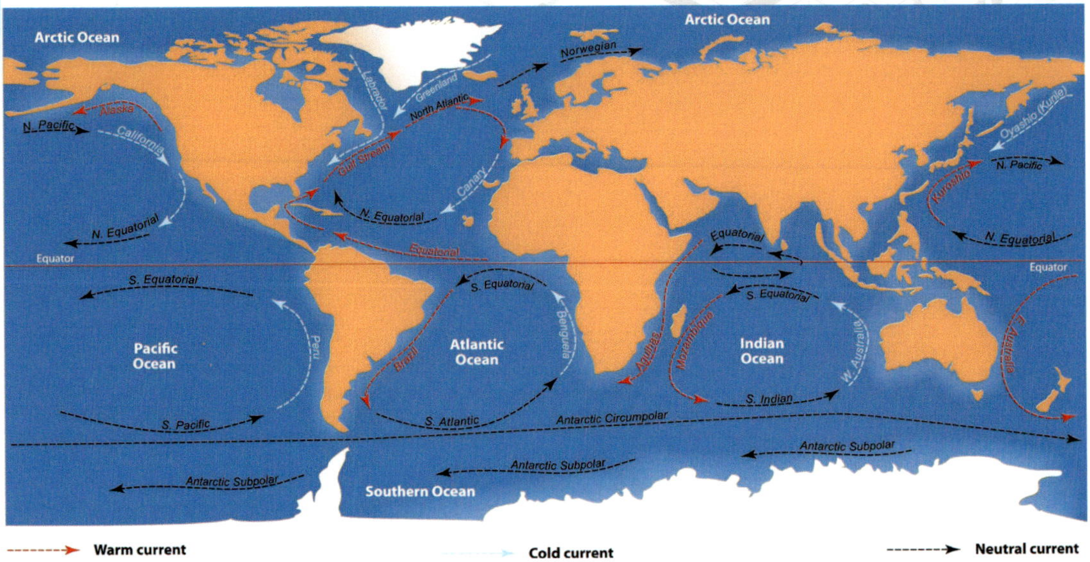

Ocean currents impact weather on land and sea.

a set pattern. Cold, salty water sinks deeper into the ocean. As it sinks, warmer water flows from nearby to take its place. This simple process affects currents around the world.

Ocean currents take place on a global scale. Huge amounts of water slowly shift around Earth. For instance, cold water from the Arctic flows away from the North Pole. Warm water is drawn toward the North Pole, where it cools. Patterns like this occur in all the world's oceans.

These currents affect the temperature of Earth. Because ocean currents move hot and cold water in set patterns, we can predict ocean temperatures. The temperature of this moving water affects the climate and weather all over Earth. This is because the temperature of air in the atmosphere changes due to flowing water in the oceans.

Winds also cause currents on the surface of the oceans. For example, the Gulf Stream is a major ocean current caused by wind. It flows from the Gulf of Mexico, next to Texas and Florida, up around the East Coast of the United States, and all the way to Europe. The Gulf Stream carries warm water to the coasts of colder regions.

This warm water results in higher temperatures than you might expect in parts of Europe. Take the case of London. The capital of Great Britain is as far north as Canada. However, on a typical winter night in London, the temperature doesn't drop below freezing. This is due to the warm water in the nearby ocean that was carried by the Gulf Stream.

THE WATER CYCLE

The oceans are also important because of their role in the water cycle. The water cycle describes how water changes form. The movement of water in this cycle is necessary for life on Earth.

About 97 percent of Earth's water is salt water in the oceans. The remaining 3 percent is in lakes, rivers, and glaciers; is stored underground; and is in the atmosphere. Much of this is fresh water. Fresh water is important because most land animals need it to live.

Earth's water is always moving. As the water moves, it affects the weather and climate. Rain and snow fall from the sky, keeping plants and animals alive. This precipitation is part of the water cycle.

In this image, it is easy to see just how much of Earth's surface is covered by water.

Evaporation

There is no real first step in the water cycle. All the steps happen at the same time. At any moment, most water on Earth is stored in oceans. As the oceans are heated by sunlight, some water from the surface evaporates. Evaporation occurs when liquid water is heated until it becomes water vapor. Water vapor is water that is in the form of a gas. Water vapor is invisible—you can't see it. However, it is in the air all around you. Humidity is a measure of how much water vapor is in the air, and it affects the weather and climate.

Most evaporation occurs on the surface of oceans, but some also occurs on land. Water in lakes and rivers evaporates as it is warmed by the sun. Water that falls to the ground as rain and snow also evaporates.

Water vapor in the atmosphere is a greenhouse gas. Like carbon dioxide, it traps heat from the sun in the atmosphere. Different amounts of water vapor exist in different places. In the desert, the humidity is usually quite low. Along the coast, humidity is usually high. The air is full of water vapor that evaporated from the nearby ocean.

Condensation

Water vapor in the atmosphere eventually condenses. Condensation is when water vapor, a gas, becomes liquid once again. Condensation occurs when water vapor cools down. In the atmosphere, condensation results in clouds. Clouds are water droplets and tiny ice crystals.

You can also see condensation in everyday life. When you pour a glass of ice water, water droplets form on the outside of

A cold glass causes water vapor from the air to condense on it.

the glass. This, too, is condensation. The coolness of the glass creates condensation from the water vapor in the air.

Precipitation

After condensing, water exists in the atmosphere as droplets in clouds. When these droplets are small, they can stay in the sky. As they clump together and grow bigger, the water droplets get heavier. Eventually, they drop toward the ground as rain, snow, or hail. This is precipitation.

Hail falls when water droplets freeze after forming in clouds.

Once the precipitation hits the ground, the water cycle continues. Most precipitation falls into the ocean. From there, it eventually evaporates again. Some precipitation falls onto land. This water moves due to gravity. Gravity is the force that pulls everything down toward the center of Earth. Gravity is why precipitation falls. It is also why water flows downhill.

Flowing water can go many different places. Some joins rivers or lakes. Other water flows underground. Groundwater is an important source of water for plants and animals. Plants use their roots to draw it up. Humans dig wells to tap into groundwater to drink. The water cycle is what lets plants and animals live.

MAKE YOUR OWN MODEL OF THE WATER CYCLE

To make your own model of the water cycle, all you need is paper and something to draw with. You can sketch with a pencil or color a picture with markers, crayons, or colored pencils. First, draw an ocean on one side of the bottom half of your paper and land on the other. Make sure the top half of your paper is left blank for the sky. On the side with land, draw a mountain and a lake as well. The water cycle occurs differently depending on the setting.

Making your own drawing can help you see the water cycle in action.

Next, draw evaporation occurring in the ocean and lake. Water vapor is invisible, but you can use squiggly lines going from the water to the sky to show water vapor rising. Label these lines "evaporation."

Then, draw clouds in the sky. Label them "condensation." From the clouds, draw precipitation falling down. You can draw rain in some places and snow falling at the top of the mountain, where it is colder. Label these "precipitation."

Now you've finished a simple model of the water cycle. The steps of the water cycle are occurring all the time around you. It causes precipitation like rain, snow, and hail. If the water cycle didn't occur, climate and weather would be very different on Earth.

Test Yourself

1. What process of the water cycle does heat from the sun cause?
2. Where would you draw arrows to show where precipitation that falls onto land goes?
3. What is the name of the force that makes precipitation flow downhill?
4. What percentage of Earth's water is in its oceans?

Answers:

1. Sunlight heats up liquid water, causing it to evaporate.
2. Precipitation flows downhill to the lake, the ocean, or under the ground. It also evaporates from the land's surface.
3. Gravity causes water and snow to move downhill.
4. About 97 percent of water on Earth is in the oceans at any one time.

Glossary

accurate Correct; exact.

air pressure The weight of air pressing down on Earth at a given spot. Air pressure changes depending on things like temperature and how high up a place is.

carbon dioxide A gas that is in air. Carbon dioxide is a greenhouse gas that contributes to climate change.

climate The typical weather of a place. Scientists use data from long ranges of time to figure out climate.

condensation The change of water from a gas to a liquid.

evaporation The change of water from a liquid to a gas.

fossil fuels Coal, crude oil, and natural gas; fossil fuels produce energy like electricity, but they also cause climate change by producing greenhouse gases.

greenhouse gases Gases that contribute to climate change by trapping heat in Earth's atmosphere.

humidity The amount of water vapor in the air.

invisible Impossible to see.

model A tool scientists use to show and test their ideas. Models can be things you can touch or hold, like a Styrofoam model of the solar system. They can also be charts, graphs, computer programs, or mathematical equations.

precipitation Rain, snow, sleet, or hail.

vary To be different.

water vapor Water in the form of a gas.

Further Information

BOOKS

Carson, Mary Kay. *Inside Weather.* Sterling Inside Series. New York, NY: Sterling Children's Books, 2011.

Dykstra, Mary. *Climate Change and Extreme Storms.* Climate Change Series. Minneapolis, MN: Lerner Publishing Group, 2019.

Furgang, Kathy. *Everything Weather: Facts, Photos, and Fun That Will Blow Your Mind!* National Geographic Kids Everything Series. Washington, DC: National Geographic Society, 2012.

WEBSITES

Climate Basics for Kids

https://www.c2es.org/content/climate-basics-for-kids

The Center for Climate and Energy Solutions explains climate change and lists ways you can help stop it.

Global Ice Viewer

https://climate.nasa.gov/interactives/global-ice-viewer

NASA shows how glaciers and ice sheets are shrinking around the world due to climate change.

VIDEOS

The Greenhouse Effect

https://youtu.be/VYMjSule0Bw

The Environmental Protection Agency describes how greenhouse gases cause the greenhouse effect in this video.

Meteorologist Ryan Davidson Explains Weather Maps

https://youtu.be/9NZz-EeveJ8

A meteorologist created this video to explain weather forecasting and how to read a weather map.

The Water Cycle

https://youtu.be/al-do-HGuIk

Watch as NBC Learn and the National Science Foundation talk about the water cycle and its importance.

Index

Page numbers in **boldface** refer to images.

About the Author

Derek Miller is an educator from Salisbury, Maryland. He is the author of more than a dozen books, including *Science Investigators: Investigating Energy Through Modeling* and *Science Investigators: Investigating Space Through Modeling*. In his free time, Miller likes to read and travel with his wife.